D1570844

THIS BOOK BELONGS TO

_____

13-Digit ISBN: 978-1604337846
10-Digit ISBN: 1604337842

This book may be ordered by mail from the publisher. Please include $5.99 for postage and handling. Please support your local bookseller first!

Books published by Cider Mill Press Book Publishers are available at special discounts for bulk purchases in the United States by corporations, institutions, and other organizations. For more information, please contact the publisher.

Cider Mill Press Book Publishers
"Where good books are ready for press"
PO Box 454
12 Spring Street
Kennebunkport, Maine 04046

Visit us online!
cidermillpress.com

Cover design by Annalisa Sheldahl
Interior design by Alicia Freile, Tango Media
Typography: AT Sackers Classic Roman Light, Georgia and Voluta Script Pro
Image Credits: O-band image: First office White House photo of Mrs. John F. Kennedy, Mark Shaw, (Library of Congress, LC-USZ62-21796); Front endpapers: John F. Kennedy home, Brookline, MA, Carol M. Highsmith (Library of Congress, LC-HS503-695); Jacqueline Bouvier Kennedy and John F. Kennedy celebrate their wedding, Toni Frissell (Library of Congress, LC-DIG-ds-07095); Jacqueline Kennedy Onassis on board the Landmark Express, Helen Hayes (Wikimedia Commons); First Lady Jacqueline Kennedy with daughter Caroline, Keystone Pictures USA (Alamy Stock Photo, E0W1RF); Back endpapers: aerial view of Jacqueline Kennedy Onassis Reservoir, NYC (pisaphotography/ Shutterstock.com); all other images, John F. Kennedy Presidential Library and Museum.

Printed in China
1 2 3 4 5 6 7 8 9 0
First Edition

JACQUELINE KENNEDY ONASSIS

NOTEBOOK

CIDER MILL PRESS

BOOK PUBLISHERS

KENNEBUNKPORT, MAINE

Introduction

BY BARBARA A. PERRY, WHITE BURKETT MILLER
CENTER PROFESSOR OF ETHICS & INSTITUTIONS,
DIRECTOR OF PRESIDENTIAL STUDIES AT THE
MILLER CENTER, UNIVERSITY OF VIRGINIA

*A*t her funeral in May of 1994, Jacqueline
Kennedy Onassis's brother-in-law, Senator
Edward Kennedy, said of her: "No one else
looked like her, spoke like he, wrote like her, or was
so original in the way she did things." Yet "she never
wanted pubic notice ...," he recalled. Ironically, she
became the most publicly noticed woman in the
world from the moment her husband was elected
president in 1960. Her courage in the aftermath of
President John F. Kennedy's assassination seared
her image in the public consciousness.

Unlike most modern First Ladies, Mrs. Kennedy
eschewed writing a memoir and never revealed her
innermost secrets to a public audience. Yet, in 2011,

Caroline Kennedy released her mother's 1964 oral history. These eight hours of frank conversations, excerpted in this notebook, provide windows into Jacqueline Kennedy's psyche and personality.

From her youth, Jacqueline Bouvier loved reading, especially poetry, which she began memorizing and writing in elementary school. At age ten she produced and illustrated a delightful poem, "Sea Joy," about her desire to live by the sea. Attending Miss Porter's School in Farmington, Connecticut, Jacqueline wrote for the school newspaper and developed her passion for art and literature. Although a self-described tomboy in her youth, she blossomed into a beautiful debutante, attracting boys with her ethereal voice.

For college, Jacqueline chose Vassar but found its campus in upstate New York stultifying. She spent her junior year in Paris, learning to speak fluent French and absorbing every detail of French culture. As she noted, it was the best year of her young life and confirmed her lifelong thirst for knowledge. After graduation from George Washington University, she remained in the nation's capital as an aspiring journalist and photographer.

In 1951 a mutual friend introduced her to Jack Kennedy, then a U.S. Senator from Massachusetts. No sparks flew at the introductory dinner party, but a year later Jacqueline and Jack discovered a chemistry in their shared interests, including love of poetry. They married in 1953, and Jacqueline Kennedy settled into life as a political wife. For their first wedding anniversary, she composed a poem about her husband, based on Stephen Vincent Benét's "John Brown's Body." She also served as Jack's research assistant for his Pulitzer Prize-winning book, *Profiles in Courage*.

By the time JFK was well into his quest for the 1960 Democratic presidential nomination, Jacqueline was pregnant with John Jr. Curtailing her campaign appearances, she wrote a column, "Campaign Wife," published in newspapers across the country. After her husband's election, the new First Lady worried about family privacy in the White House fish bowl, but she found life there far more enjoyable than she envisioned.

Even before the 1961 inauguration, Jacqueline decided that her focus as First Lady would center on restoring the White House to its historic authenticity. As she told NBC correspondent Sander Vanocur, the Executive Mansion belonged to all Americans, and each presidential spouse should leave her stamp on its history. In her short 1,036 days there, Mrs. Kennedy fulfilled that goal, making each state room a model for decorative arts, painting, and sculpture. She also founded the White House Historical Association and produced a guidebook for visitors as well as a brief history of presidents in the White

House. At the height of the Cold War, Mrs. Kennedy made the President's home a shining symbol of American freedom and democracy.

The First Lady stood by her husband during the most harrowing moments of the free world's conflict with communism, including the failed Bay of Pigs invasion. During 1962's Cuban Missile Crisis, she told Jack that she would refuse evacuation. Her choice was to die with her family if a nuclear conflagration engulfed Washington. She was indeed by her husband's side when he died, but not as the result of war with the Soviets. Sitting next to him on November 22, 1963, Mrs. Kennedy witnessed the horrific assassination of her husband by gunshot as their convertible drove past the Texas School Book Depository.

After planning his Lincolnesque funeral, the former First Lady devoted the next thirty years to her children. In 1968 she married Greek shipping magnate Aristotle Onassis. After his death seven years later, she became a literary editor of biographies, art books, and memoirs, including Michael Jackson's. Mrs. Onassis embraced her public role as a historic preservationist, even giving news conferences to save New York City's Grand Central Station.

As Senator Edward Kennedy concluded in his eulogy, "She made a rare and noble contribution to the American spirit.... She graced our history."

One doesn't know if one

LEADS IN THE RIGHT DIRECTION

or not, but one hopes one does.

— *Oral history interview with historian Arthur Schlesinger Jr.*
(March 24, 1964)

Even a more

FORMIDABLE TASK

than housing tomorrow's
students will be providing
them with good teachers.

—*"Campaign Wife" column (Fall 1960)*

*President and Mrs. Kennedy with their children,
John Jr. and Caroline (August 4, 1962)*

If we don't care about our past we can't have very much hope for our future. We've all heard that it's too late, or that it has to happen, that it's inevitable. But I don't think that's true. Because I think if there is a great effort,

EVEN IF IT'S THE ELEVENTH HOUR,

then you can succeed, and I know that's what we'll do.

— Remarks made at a press conference for the Committee to Save Grand Central Station (January 30, 1975)

I don't think the White House
ever can completely belong
to one person.

It belongs to
the people of
America.

And I think whoever lives in it,
the First Lady, should preserve its
traditions and enhance it and leave
something of herself there.

*— Interview with NBC White House Correspondent
Sander Vanocur* (October 1, 1960)

First Lady Jacqueline Kennedy playing with her children,
Caroline Bouvier Kennedy and John Fitzgerald Kennedy Jr.
(November 27, 1962)

Every first lady should do
something in this position to
HELP THE
THINGS SHE
CARES ABOUT.
I would hope that when I leave
here, I will have done something.

*— Interview with NBC White House Correspondent
Sander Vanocur* (March 24, 1961)

*President John F. Kennedy greets First Lady Jacqueline Kennedy
and daughter Caroline on their return from a trip to Italy
(August 31, 1962)*

I had always wanted to write.
I think I thought I could write

THE GREAT
AMERICAN
NOVEL.

*— Interview with NBC White House Correspondent
Sander Vanocur* (October 1, 1960)

It's funny. I used to worry about going into the White House...And then once you got in it, I mean, you were just so happy for him, then you found out that it was really

THE HAPPIEST TIME OF MY LIFE.

It was when we were the closest —
I didn't realize the physical closeness
of having his office in the same
building and seeing him so many
times a day.

— Oral history interview with historian Arthur Schlesinger Jr.
(March 23, 1964)

Jacqueline Bouvier Kennedy and John F. Kennedy celebrate their wedding with family in Newport, Rhode Island (September 12, 1953)

I loved it more than any year of my life. Being away from home gave me a chance to look at myself with a jaundiced eye. I learned not to be ashamed of

A REAL HUNGER FOR KNOWLEDGE,

something I had always tried to hide, and I came home glad to start in here again but with a love for Europe that I am afraid will never leave me.

— *Remarks made by Jacqueline Bouvier upon returning from her junior year of college abroad in Paris* (circa 1950)

I was never any different
once I was in the White House
than I was before, but the press
made you different. Suddenly,
everything that'd been a liability
before...all the things that
I'd always done,

SUDDENLY
BECAME
WONDERFUL

because anything the First Lady
does that's different, everyone
seizes on.

— Oral history interview with historian Arthur Schlesinger Jr.
(March 23, 1964)

First Lady Jacqueline Kennedy riding horses with
her children at Wexford, the Kennedys' Virginia home
(November 19, 1962)

I'd always had this mania before about making my children learn French because I saw how that other language

ABSOLUTELY DOUBLED MY LIFE,

and made you able to meet all those people...but I said "I'm going to make my children learn Spanish as their second language."...[Because] really, we should turn to this hemisphere.

— Oral history interview with historian Arthur Schlesinger Jr.
(March 24, 1964)

I think it's so good to be able
to able to

FORGIVE QUICKLY.

That's a quality that Jack liked in
me....I think it's hard for men to
make up first in a family, in
a rather intimate way. But he
did that same thing.

— Oral history interview with historian Arthur Schlesinger Jr.
(March 4, 1964)

First Lady Jacqueline Kennedy at the White House Reception for
the Latin American Diplomatic Corps (March 3, 1961)

"Even if there's not room in the bomb shelter in the White House"—which I'd seen. I said "Please, then I just want to be with you on the lawn when it happens —you know—but

I JUST WANT TO BE WITH YOU,

and I want to die with you, and the children too—than live without you."

— On the Cuban Missile Crisis, in an oral history interview with historian Arthur Schlesinger Jr. (March 24, 1964)

I've often noticed that the art of children is the same for children the world over, and so of course is our love for children. I think it is good, in a world where it is quite enough to divide people, that we should

CHERISH THE LANGUAGE AND EMOTION THAT UNITES US ALL.

— Remarks made by First Lady Jacqueline Kennedy during her trip to India (March 1962)

First Lady Jacqueline Kennedy visits New Delhi, India,
with Indira Gandhi (March 14, 1962)

I think he liked that I was—I mean, he knew that I was being myself....And he married me, really, for the things that I was, but then when they didn't work out politically, he was never going to ask me to change...

BECAUSE HE WOULDN'T BE FAKE IN ANY WAY.

— Oral history interview with historian Arthur Schlesinger Jr., speaking about John F. Kennedy (June 3, 1964)

Is it not cruel to let our city die by degrees, stripped of all her proud moments, until there is nothing left of all her

HISTORY AND BEAUTY

to inspire our children? If they are not inspired by the past of our city, where will they find the strength to fight for her future?

— On saving Grand Central Station, in a letter to New York City Mayor Abraham Beame (February 24, 1975)

*Jacqueline Kennedy Onassis on board the Landmark Express,
a train chartered by the Committee To Save Grand Central
Terminal. The group took the train to Washington, D.C. ahead
of oral arguments before the Supreme Court in the case of Penn
Central Transportation Co. v. New York City, which would
decide the fate of Grand Central (April 16, 1978)*

First Lady Jacqueline Kennedy plays with daughter Caroline at the Kennedy's home in Palm Beach, Florida (January 1, 1962)

If you bungle raising your children, I don't think whatever else you do well

MATTERS VERY MUCH.

— *Interview with NBC White House Correspondent Sander Vanocur* (October 1, 1960)

I am

GRATEFUL TO
MY PARENTS

for the effort they made
to teach us foreign
languages.

— *"Campaign Wife" column* (Fall 1960)

All these people have

CONTRIBUTED SO MUCH TO OUR COUNTRY'S CULTURE;

it seems a proper courtesy to
address them in their own tongue.

—"Campaign Wife" column (Fall 1960)

First Lady Jacqueline Kennedy at the Opening of the Mona Lisa
exhibit at the National Gallery of Art, Washington, D.C.
(January 8, 1963)

I...always taught them that the White House was sort of temporary...

I'D TELL THEM LITTLE STORIES ABOUT OTHER PRESIDENTS,

and then there would be a president after Daddy, and then we would be living in Hyannis. And, you know, so they never got to think that all this was going to be forever in this power.

— On raising her children in the White House, in an oral history interview with historian Arthur Schlesinger Jr. (June 3, 1964)

First Lady Jacqueline Kennedy plays with her children on Christmas Day at the home of Colonel C. Michael Paul in Palm Beach, Florida (December 25, 1962)

I remember thinking in the White House, "What was the matter with me that I spent so much time worrying, would it ruin our marriage to get in the White House?" And here it was so happy. And then I thought,

YOU NEVER CAN KNOW WHAT WILL BE THE BEST FOR YOU.

— *Oral history interview with historian Arthur Schlesinger Jr.*
(March 23, 1964)

First Lady Jacqueline Kennedy and President John F. Kennedy attend the premiere of "Mr. President" at the National Theatre in Washington, D.C. (September 25, 1962)

About Cider Mill Press
Book Publishers

Good ideas ripen with time. From seed to harvest,
Cider Mill Press brings fine reading, information,
and entertainment together between the covers
of its creatively crafted books. Our Cider Mill
bears fruit twice a year, publishing a new crop
of titles each spring and fall.

"Where Good Books Are Ready for Press"

Visit us on the web at
www.cidermillpress.com
or write to us at
PO Box 454
12 Spring St.
Kennebunkport, Maine 04046